From Here Until Forever

From Here Until Forever

New Thought
Insights & Perspectives
On Living A Spiritual Life
In A Physical World

Essays
V. Blakeman Vaughn

© V. Blakeman Vaughn 2019
ISBN 978-0-9714359-7-1

All rights reserved. No part of this publication may be reproduced in any form without written permission of Darkhorse Press

www.darkhorsepress.com
contact@darkhorsepress.com

Table of Contents

#1	What Life's For	1
#2	The Journey	4
#3	Look At Your Life	9
#4	A Child Shall Lead Them	15
#5	Effort Versus Faith	17
#6	Healing The Past	19
#7	You Could Choose Peace	22
#8	What Is New Thought?	25
#9	Who Do I Want To Be?	32
#10	Mission and Purpose In Life	34
#11	The Gift of Now	37
#12	Has God Forgot?	41
#13	The Positive Bias of God	42
#14	The Soul-Mind	45
#15	Life-Science for Beginners	47
#16	The Deepest Voice	51
#17	From Here Until Forever	52
#18	Making Mistakes	54
#19	Moments	55
#20	Do What You Do	58
#21	Everything That Comes	60
#22	What's Important	63
#23	Before I wake	64
#24	Live Today	69

"when you want to discover the gift that nature has given to you, you must first stop blaming yourself for being who you are."

– Ravi Shankar

Introduction

A new world-paradigm is forming, and you are a part of it. You haven't come to this point in your life by accident. Everything that has happened in your life, every obstacle, every gift, has had meaning and has been called forth by your soul, your greater Self, to help yours and the world's emerging consciousness to expand, deepen, and grow.

Some of the truths and concepts you discover in this book may be different from traditions you grew up with. Whatever rings true for you personally, take that to your heart, and leave the rest for a while. Trust your own heart and intuition to know what's true for you, and important for you now, as you enter into your personal spirituality, your direct-connect with God.

I remember wondering about God when I was a child, and so my Granny taught me a simple kind of faith that I could understand, that made me feel safe and loved. She said God was all around me like the air and the sky, only bigger. I knew the sky was there forever, and God would be too. I confess I don't know much more now, about what God is, than I did then, and maybe that was a truer explanation than anything else I've learned since. I was sure that I was safe, and sure that I was loved.

As an adult, I know that God is still around me, and moving through me, but now sometimes I have confusion, doubts and nagging uncertainties about how this whole God-thing works, because the world I live in is such a tangled-up mess. I've read and studied spiritual texts, the words of mystics and Master teachers who have said that we have power over our own lives, whether we realize it or not. By the choices we make, whether conscious or unaware, we have created the world as it is, and we are creating the world that will be in the future. I have found this to be true.

I invite you to take a bold step toward a kinder and saner world. The power of change lies in how many of us are learning and growing in mindfulness and spiritual awareness. There are millions making this journey with us. Let us decide to share it together wherever our paths converge.

We are all on the journey together. Eventually we will know this, and return home to the same place, to find that we have been connected all along and sent here together at this time, for a purpose.

Now is the portal
to the vast unknown,
Now is the eternal brink
of everything
that will ever be.
To live in the present
means trusting yourself
and trusting God.

1. What Life's For

It's all about Learning. It's not about achieving. When you achieve something, what you learn is, "I can set a goal, target my thoughts and actions toward it, and accomplish it." This is part of your soul's power: that it can manifest things and events in the physical world. When Jesus said "Nothing shall be impossible to you, if you have faith" he was speaking quite literally. Whatever you desire in this world, if you focus your intention on it, move toward it mentally and physically, and believe that you can have it, you will eventually have it. The hard part is the believing.

If you have experienced success, you may believe in success more than you believe in failure. If you have experienced what we call failure, you may tend to expect it, and you may believe in it more than you believe in success. What we believe, we receive.

Another amazing and thought-provoking thing Jesus said was "Blessed are they who have not seen, and yet believe." This was a clue I think, that we do have a choice in what we believe.

We can endeavor to believe in the ways we want things to go, and they will be more likely to go those ways. Or we can focus on worry and fear that they won't go the way we want, and they probably won't. What we hold in thought materializes in our lives. We have the power to profoundly influence our lives by choosing what thoughts we maintain. The catch is, so many of our choices are made unconsciously or by habit.

Whatever your belief is, your choices will be, and your actions will mirror. You can change your life by choosing either to change your beliefs, or to change your choices and actions.

We choose what we believe we deserve, and then Life/God/the Universe unfailingly produces *whatever we believe*. Who you are now and what you have are what you chose. What you will have and who you will be in the future, you are choosing right now.

Look at your life without judging it, and ask yourself "What do I really want?" Note: the question is not "What should a person like me want?" And not "What do I want that I have a good chance of getting?" The answer you're looking for is at a deeper level than the conscious worldly mind, so listen patiently and wait. The answer may come like a thunderbolt, but more likely it will come very quietly.

Each time we achieve a difficult or lofty goal we have wanted and worked for, that feels wonderful. Our Truth is made manifest on life's stage. We learn that tangible success is one of our options, one of the many choices of our soul's power.

Success feels good, so there is a danger of becoming addicted to it, staying there and going no further. That's why your soul also seeks other options and experiences. You have come here to experience everything, to learn, and break through barriers, especially spiritual ones. This is why your soul sometimes chooses other options, such as "not succeeding" or not achieving the goal that's been set by the personality of you.

We usually call this kind of not-succeeding "failure" but that's not accurate. From this "failure" experience we always have the opportunity to learn greater truths, such as this one: "There are no failures, only learnings." This I was told by my Inner Counselor at a time when I did not want to hear it, and yet I knew it was the biggest thing I needed to learn, and I could never have learned it from success.

Contemporary spiritual writer Gary Zukav coined the

phrase "The Earth School," and I think that's a reasonable interpretation of what we're here for: primarily to learn and grow in every way, especially in spirit. But I think the term doesn't quite say enough, because I believe there is also an element of sharing the gifts, that goes along with this Earth Journey.

We have each been given a unique set of gifts. Some of them we develop, and some we don't. This means you too. It includes that talent you're embarrassed to admit, the poetry you're too shy to show anyone, the love of working with your hands with wood or stone or steel, or that secret love of rivers, or constellations, or human history, or some other seemingly unlikely thing that probably will not make you a millionaire. Yet it's been right there, quietly in the back of your heart all your life. Consider bringing it out. Maybe just in small ways at first, and see what happens. Consider honoring it. Consider sharing it.

The life you are living now is not all there is. In fact, it's a very small part of all there is. There is much more that we are unable to comprehend or even imagine it with the limitations of a human mind. Yet you have not come here without purpose, and your life has meaning that you can't see yet. Your soul knows, and from the inside of you, it gently urges you to trust and believe, move forward with faith, mindfully, honestly, and earnestly living the life you have now. Because even though your soul will have other lifetimes, you will never have this one again. The particular gifts of this life must be shared in this lifetime, or they will remain unshared for eternity.

2. The Journey

This life has often been described as a journey, and our spiritual path in life is one of discovery and growth. Some say the primary function for which we all came was to learn through experiences. We see this ancient concept in the Australian Aboriginal rite of passage from childhood to manhood that's called the "walkabout" and similar practices and tests of courage in Native American and countless other tribal traditions from every area of our planet. All of them are journeys of passage and spiritual transcendence.

The purpose of our travel through this Life is not to get somewhere, but to experience the journey itself. We already are somewhere: exactly where we need to be. The Life-journey is not about a destination or an ending point but about destiny, which is an eternal going forward that is already here, all along the way. Our manifest destiny is to live, learn, and grow throughout eternity. Forms will change, but the Life of us, the spirit that is our true Being, continues. The goal of human life is transcendence, to "extending beyond the limits of ordinary experience, beyond the limits of all past experience and knowledge."

We will learn our Life-Lessons from its challenges, problems, and whatever adventures life offers us. The main idea is not necessarily to get it right (or get it wrong) but simply to *get it*.

Most of the world's religions believe in some form of reincarnation or eternal life, that there is a higher Life after this mortal one, in another form or way. Many faiths believe that we may return for many lifetimes on earth. I believe in the possibility of this, it makes sense to me. It does seem unimaginable, to get it all, in one short life. But whether it will be one lifetime or many, we get plenty of opportunities to learn each of our soul's chosen lessons, especially the important ones. And how can we recognize which ones are most important? That's easy. They keep coming up.

When we were learning our ABC's, we had to repeat them many many times before we really "knew them by heart." This is one of the ways we learn, by repetition. That's why the same old self-defeating, self-sabotaging, self-limiting patterns keep on turning up to challenge us over and over – to give us more chances to learn our way past them, to transcend, and move to the next level.

"I thought I was past that!" I hear myself say. *"I guess not. Here it is again."* Wearing a different hat, showing up in a different person, another circumstance basically the same.

The Victim/martyr trap is the one I've personally struggled with, from almost-insignificant little events to major life-decisions. It's also called "Door-mat" syndrome, "People-pleaser," "codependent" and other names.

Most of my young life I was not strong enough or brave enough to stand up and say No. Or Yes. Or whatever I really wanted. I was afraid tell the real truth because I thought it was not what the other person wanted to hear, and if I gave them the "wrong" answer I would have to pay a terrible price because of it. I learned this as a child. It never was actually true, but for as long as I believed it, it seemed to prove true again and again.

This is a common habit for us all. A "dishonesty for self-defense." Being honest means being vulnerable, that's scary. And yet if we never show our true self to anyone, no one can really know or really love, *us*. They can only love or not-love, respect or not-respect, some public version of us, while our authentic self remains unknown.

When I woke up one day and began to realize some things I was still believing, and challenge them, they began to change.

I eventually learned to practice a quiet appropriate way to speak my truth *as I see it,* and ask for what I really wanted instead of what I thought I might have the best chance to get. Surprisingly, and soon, things began to *routinely work out better.* I ended up a stronger person, and I received more respect as well. I'm not saying this is easy, it's not. But like anything else, it gets easier with practice, and it does work.

We don't recognize the self-limiting scenarios and pre-programmed sub-plots in our lives until we look back over our shoulder and see the patterns repeating. I can tell that Im growing, because now I'm seeing the pattern sooner. I stop and challenge it: *"What's really going on here?"* I pull back for an instant and recognize that *I have the choice to break free of it this time. Maybe not every time, but this time.*

It *is possible.* I have the choice to change the course of events by changing my relationship to them. I can't force things to change, but I can choose to change how I see things, as the person I want to be, as how I want to see myself. *I can recognize that my opinion of me is much more powerful in my life than their opinion of me. When I see this, amazingly, things start to change themselves.*

What we give our attention to, grows. That's simply the way universal Energy works. If we focus on thinking about how we've been mistreated (and realistically, everyone has been at some time) we attract more of that unwanted experience into our present and future life.

When I finally got sick and tired of that same blind-loop, tired of being poor-pitiful-me, I made a decision: to refuse to expect the worst, to refuse to worry and obsess over things, to NOT invest emotion in them, (even though that was hard) *and to refuse to keep on reviewing my misery thoughts like a dog gnawing on a bone.*

Instead I decided to consciously shift my attention to some other, more pleasant thought. I took charge and ownership of my own mind and its habits.

I reasoned, *If I can quit smoking, I can quit obsessing. I can do or not do what I choose and claim for myself.* I still remember the very day and the exact place I was standing when the shocking realization hit me:

My misery thoughts don't do anything to the people or circumstances that hurt me, yet they are still hurting ME. The difference is that now it's not that person or experience that's hurting me, it's ME that's hurting me, because I've been giving those ugly feelings a prime parking place, right up-front in my thoughts and my life!

We don't have to do that to ourselves. Why not try this: next time something makes you feel angry or hurt, *pull your attention away from that,* and park your mental focus someplace else. Any pleasant thought will do. Call up a mental picture of some blessing you do have, some happy memory from when you were ten years old, if you have some there. Think of some beautiful place you've seen, something funny you saw on TV, anything that's good in your life, or something good you hope will come.

Shift-focus your thoughts away from the anger and resentment. When you hold onto those (perfectly natural) emotions and negative thoughts, that does not change the offending person or thing, it just keeps on making YOU feel worse. Do you deserve that? Of course you don't. Decide to make hurtful, hateful, or painful thoughts go, *by choice.* Choose the happier mood you know you deserve.

Build a new habit. When the misery-thought rudely shoves its way back in again (and it will, repeatedly) yank your attention away again, and park your thoughts in a better place, again. This works brilliantly. In a few days (or sometimes in a few minutes) you'll start to notice that things are starting to change. A relationship, problem, or whatever it was, has somehow begun to untangle and resolve itself. As soon as you are different on the inside, this will have a powerful effect on whatever is going on, on the outside.

I'm not free of all my old patterns. I have a lot more to learn, and that of course is what keeps life interesting. But now when I see the old thought-patterns coming up, I can decide to make other choices, ones that are happier *for me.*

A profound book "A Course In Miracles" says "There are no accidents and no coincidences. Everything that happens to us has been called into our lives by us, and we receive just as we have asked."

There is one thing I know for sure, and life proves it consistently: *We are what we believe we are.* When we choose to be helpless by allowing ourselves to believe we are helpless, in an instant, we become helpless. If we choose to believe we're the victims of other people's influence, we will be. *But we always have the choice.*

Different as we are, we are all expressions of God, and the rules are the same for everybody. We have been put here together to learn from each other. There is no easy cop-out, we either take possession of our own life and live it with honesty, responsibility and awareness, or we don't. We must make mistakes, because that's how we learn. No human life is going to be all easy, so we can only do the best we can. Living a life of honesty is a big responsibility, but in the log run, it has big rewards.

To really love life and live it with spirit and joy takes courage, commitment, and conscious co-creation with God. This is an astonishing, ever-changing, wonderful journey that never ends, and you've got a ticket to ride.

3. Look At Your Life

Every so often, stop and take a Look at your life. What are you choosing? What is showing up that you did not really want? There is a gift in it. Look and try to see what it is. The gift always contains a learning, which if recognized, empowers you to break free and let go of a hurtful or self-defeating pattern you have been repeating. It may be obvious, or it may be very subtle. Your soul is letting you know it's time for you to grow a little, or a lot. Look for the learning, recognize it, and you will know what you need to do to get back on-center in your path.

This happens continually in our lives. We are here to learn and grow spiritually. Your soul came here with its own list of projects, unknown to this personality that seems to be you. Who you are is greater than this personality or this lifetime, but this personality and this lifetime are important and sacred.

Your soul and mine and all souls, have come here on a contract with God that: (1) You shall have experiences in the physical world in which to learn and grow. (2) God shall provide all the strength and help and substance and guidance you will ever need, with which to do this. (3) The access point from which you reach and manifest all this is available from inside of you.

It's not necessary to go to any particular place, belong to any particular church, or follow any particular dogma in order to access God and spiritual guidance. That is already provided for you. Seek and find, ask and receive. The door opens from the inside.

You cannot possibly ever be where God is not. As every drop of water in the ocean is not just a part of the ocean, it IS the ocean, so too are you of God. You are a part of God, and God is a part of you, but this is not two things, it only appears to be, in the mind. Whether you choose to accept and receive Him/Her or not, God is always and eternally, immediately, right where you are, right now.

Why then does anybody ever fail? Why then do some people kill? The "Catch-22" of the contract is this: God has empowered us with free choice. We can and do create the events and circumstances of our lives, but our choices are influenced unawarely by deeply embedded unconscious thoughts and beliefs. Most of them were planted in our childhood, when were too young to weigh their value or determine their truth or untruth.

And so we may have unknowingly and innocently believed that the values and limitations of the past, or of the physical world, are all there is. But we are grown now. We can choose to believe that God/Spirit is real, present, available, and greater than the physical world, for this is the truth that has the power to set us free.

Whichever you choose to believe, you will hold in your thoughts, and so express and manifest in your life. Many people have chosen greed, cruelty, insanity, even murder. They are free to make their choices, and receive the consequences of the choices they make. You are also free to choose those things, or choose differently.

We are on this journey together; that is the truth. No one is alone, and if we feel we are, it's because we have closed life's doors and windows ourselves, usually in order to feel safe. We ARE safe, we can trust God. But so many of the world's rules have made us doubt that.

God is greater than the world, and aware of every creature and thing, every expression of life upon it. You matter enormously to God, and even if you think you don't matter to anyone on earth, you could be wrong about that too. Ask for help and be willing, truly willing to accept it, in whatever form it comes. Share the love you have, and it will be returned to you multiplied.

New Thought movement writers say, "Each time you have a fearful thought, an angry or resentful thought, a lonely thought, a distressed and discouraged thought – stop yourself, and choose a new thought instead."

We can't stop all the hurtful or frightening thoughts from coming into our minds, but we do not have to give them harbor there. We must live in the world, but as a very wise teacher once said, we can *"Be not OF the world."*

We own our mind, no one else does, and no one else can. We absolutely have the power and ability to choose and change our thoughts. In time, every situation changes to match our held thought about it. This is the simple miracle of faith.

The hard part is choosing and holding firm to that true thought and belief, in spite of the habits, opinions, and seeming "evidence" of the physical world. If we could see it as God does, we would know that the physical world is just a backdrop that's constantly being changed by ourselves with the natural power of our own minds, but when we don't know this, we settle for less than life is ready and willing to give.

Try a new way – choose to knowingly, awarely, and intentionally, hold your thought and vision in faith, then trust God and *watch what happens.* The real, substantive, essential life of you is not physical. The authentic life of you is spiritual, made manifest physically in this world in order to experience, learn, and grow through the journey.

You can choose joy. Seek it, find it, give it, share it, and you will receive the consequences of that. You can start where you are right now; there's no application form, no fees, and no entrance exam. You can choose love, peace, health, prosperity, whatever you want, and if you hold those things in your heart and mind with faith, they must ultimately manifest in your life.

Does this mean you won't have challenges, sadness,

feelings of loneliness? Never have lessons in healing, never have physical death? No, it simply means that in this life, whatever you seek, either consciously or habitually, you will find, for better or for worse. Know this, and act on it, and know that the God of the universe whatever name you call Him/Her by, wants only good for you, but will not force it on you or refuse you any choice, if you choose something else.

That's how the universe works. God rarely interferes with the laws of the universe, for they are God's own laws. And yet, at any time, God can, and sometimes does, and we are given something more, or different, than what we thought we wanted or dreamed we could have. When that happens, this is the unexpected and undeserved gift of blessing that we call Grace.

So it becomes the challenge of every human being, now at this time in the evolution of the species, to move beyond the old perceived limitations of the material, and progress into the spiritual new frontier. Humanity is God's marvelous experiment. We have been given the power to choose and create our world, and knowingly or not, we have done that. The world we have right now is the one we have made, often without realizing. If this is not the world we want, we can change it, for we are recreating it right now. What we will have tomorrow is what we are choosing and building today.

To build the world we want instead of what we have created in the past, first we must recognize and accept responsibility for this truth: God will always give us what we ask for, whether we ask consciously or carelessly. So be awake and aware of what you are holding in your thoughts and in your heart, for these will create the events and of your life, good or bad, as you have chosen.

Keep in touch with your soul. Make this your most important line of communication. However you do it, at church, at home, with meditation, intuition, prayer, with quiet time alone, with walks in the forest or by the sea, or moments of meditation or solitude wherever you are. Be still and listen for the still small voice within yourself and trust what your heart knows. Your conscious mind is intended to be its servant, not its master. Your mind is a powerful tool and instrument, but *you are much more than your mind.*

Keep in touch with your soul and with your Spirit Within, that still small voice of your Inner Counselor. You will be supported and loved through everything that comes.

There is an open invitation that is immediate and eternal, to receive and accept complete forgiveness for every "sin" and "mistake" you ever thought you made, and begin again fresh, right where you are, right now. You are still wanted and precious to the God that made you and gave you life. God has promised this, and God always keeps promises.

4. A Child Shall Lead Them

In some ways we are wiser as children than we are as adults. When we were children, we knew what we wanted, from moment to moment. We knew what mattered to us.

We were born 100% authentic and open. As we were learning about life, everything was new. Our pain was more intense, and our joy more total and glorious, and everything in between was fresh and wonderful. But as we grew up, we started having to consider too many other things: like how we looked, and how we might be judged, and whether our value or the value of a thing we loved would be enough, and if we might be making a mistake.

As we adapted to the adult world, we learned to fear failing so much that all too often we decided not to try. All of life's wonders were still available to us, even more than before, but that innocent faith was gone. For many of us, the early dependent years of childhood were confusing, painful, sometimes even abusive. Our sense of Self may have taken a beating then, and now it's still trying to hide and heal. So we enter into adulthood with a lot of unlearning to do.

The primary work of life, our essential assignment here, is to experience, to learn, and to grow always more complete, more complex. But if we are to do that without being overwhelmed, we must also learn how to forgive, how to let go, how to trust, how to become simple again.

It's as if, in sleep we had received the secrets of the universe, and then on waking, forgot. So now we begin again in ignorance, with a vision that's fearful and unclear.

Because we have failed before and fear to fail again,

we hold our spirit back, trying to make sure we get things right. And yet within us there is still the remembrance of the dream: that *somewhere there was truth, and order, and instead of a struggle, life played itself out like the dance children dance in the summer rain.*

The remembrance of what once we knew with a pure knowing, how the universe had unfolded all of its secrets spontaneously, in perfect order, complexity, and simplicity before our bright, eager, curious, uncluttered minds. It was all there. It had always been there. We knew with perfect knowing before we were born, but we forgot. It is the task of life to learn again.

In this world, most of us are drowning in too much stress, too many possessions, too much entertainment, too much work, and too much multi-tasking. Is there really nothing important enough for us to actually stop and look at it? And focus on one thing at a time? In spite of all our "stuff" and constant striving for more and better stuff, inside we know that our material-stuff has very little of real Substance, of real value.

It's easy to lose ourselves in all the complexity and hurry around, busy but without purpose. We don't see because we don't look. We don't hear because we don't listen. We search for the right path without realizing that every path is ours. There is no predetermined path, there is guidance, but it is our own will and thought that take us were we go. And more than any other time in history, many of us feel as if we are "going it alone."

Yet it is impossible not to be connected to God, the universe, and each other. Separation is an illusion, but loneliness is very real when we choose to believe in separateness. In truth we are connected and intimately infused, each into each, and all into all, whether we are aware of it or not. Every human mind is directly connected to the Mind of God; it has never been otherwise.

But we wake and forget.

A child listens to the sounds of a summer night, and hears the music of the universe.

The songs of insects, the winds, the creaking of branches and whispering of leaves, and all the little familiar noises of the quiet house. All of the sounds, now together, then one by one.

The crickets trace their madrigals on the lines and spaces of the vast velvet darkness. The child closes her eyes and sees the colors and patterns of the sounds, winding and unwinding in her willing mind. The father in the same house worries about paying the bills and hears nothing at all, he sees nothing at all but empty darkness.

You could say, rightly, that the child is innocent of worries, as adults cannot be. It's true that we cannot be innocent of our complexity, but we can choose what we give our best time and thoughts to.

So I choose to put away my work and worry for an hour at twilight, so I can sit in the warm dark aliveness and just listen. When I do, I can still hear the music.

The music of the universe is still here. Be still in the Presence, and you will hear it.

5. Effort vs. Endeavor

Looking back over the experiences of my life up to now, I discover that I have achieved a lot more by faith than I have by effort. Work is a factor of course; good work is always worthwhile, and it gives you pride and a sense of accomplishment. Honest work always makes you stronger and you feel better about yourself, whereas waiting and hoping for a lucky break gives you too much idle time to dwell on old fears and past disappointments. Waiting and hoping in a state of uncertainty will always bring you feelings of helplessness about your life, while positive action is generally beneficial to both body and spirit. Faith is stronger than either hope or work, and it may prove to be stronger than anything else on earth.

The basic law of the universe is "What you believe, you receive." Simple, effective, and absolute. Take time every so often to look at your casual thoughts to see what you are believing - it might not be what you really want to receive.

When you have a strong earnest desire, that's a gift. When it's a deep quiet one that lingers, whispers to you when you're falling asleep, or comes to you as the first thought in the morning slipping into your mind just before you wake – that's your spirit talking to you. That's a gift asking permission to be given. A calling.

But you've got to set yourself in motion in order to let it come. You've got to go for it – put your heart out there. Put your body on the line and when the starter's gun goes off, run the best race you can, and believe, no matter what the odds are, that you might win. If you throw your heart out in front of you and try to catch up with it, you will run a glorious race, a better race than you ever dreamed you could, and in truth, you might win. One thing is certain: when you give your best to what your heart asks for, then no matter what your number is at the finish line, you know in your heart that you have won.

God's gifts are made manifest in our lives not by effort but by Grace, and endeavor helps them take form. Our part in this partnership is to faithfully do the work that is ours to do this day, and trust God for the outcome. When we do, the result often turns out to be different and better than the one we had imagined or planned.

Effort can be sporadic, wearying, and frustrating. But endeavor is something else. Endeavor is a fully focused commitment, a kind of action that is made out of patience, dedication and firm faith. The great teacher Jesus said, "Believe you have received it, and it shall be yours." Faith is the winner's edge. It makes all the difference in the world.

6. Healing The Past

All along our path from birth to wisdom we will receive wounds from other human beings. Big one, small ones, some done with the intention to hurt or control us, some "for our own good" and some without any conscious intention at all. Often they are done by people we love, or people who love us, with no awareness that their acts could damage so deeply.

The wounds of our childhood engrave patterns of belief and expectation about life that cut deep into our vulnerable young hearts and minds. They stay there, below the surface of our awareness, so that we live out these same old patterns of beliefs over and over. Years later the same traps and pitfalls reappear, again and again, but in new forms and different circumstances.

When we investigate Life on our own terms, and we read psychology books or we study Truth Teachings and sacred texts, we begin to see things differently. Then the struggle begins against the quicksand-pit of false beliefs and untruths, embedded for half a lifetime at the bottom of our mind. Now we have begun to recognize it. Looking back over ten or twenty years, we can see the familiar traps and stuck-places repeating over and over, just in new costumes or new places with the same old pattern underneath. Once we realize this, we are ready to begin to change our "luck" in life, and profoundly change our future.

There are many wonderful God-given writings and messengers to help us find our way out of the darkness of the past and into the light and unlimited possibility that is our birthright. We read and practice, as best we can, what our books and teachers and ministers recommend but sometimes even though the chains of those childhood mislearnings become visible, they still remain intact. We struggle even more as we realize our misdirection, and we endeavor to change it. Yet we may still find ourselves in bad situations, being misused by coworkers, or family, or bosses, or strangers. Why? And why are we still asking ourselves "Why didn't I see that coming?"

It is only by healing that we find release from the past, when we see truly and with certainty that the past has no real power over us. The truth is, nothing in the past has any power over us, except when we believe it does. Believing gives power to a thing, but the power itself is within us, and always has been.

When we take back our power from the past, we claim the right to a new present and a new future. As long as we keep on believing the "stories," the lies we learned in the past, the past will keep on repeating in the present. There is no future except the one we are creating in this moment, now. When we change what we deeply believe, everything begins to change.

Knowing is important, but believing is at the center of everything. What we believe, plays out and becomes true in our lives. We create the circumstances of our lives by what we choose to believe, even if we live much of our lives without even realizing what we are "buying into" unaware of what we are unconsciously believing.

When we begin to be aware of our thoughts and beliefs, we can begin to take dominion over them, and to make better, happier choices for our lives. Problems will still come, but they will be recognized as opportunities through which we can heal and grow. They will not be cured simply by understanding, by intellect, by actions, or even by prayer, alone. There can be no cure without healing, and healing is a decision, an inner action that changes us. It is this kind of healing that releases us from the past. It requires the belief that it is not only possible, but right and natural, and that *we deserve it*. One of the common lies we learned as children is that we were somehow undeserving, not good enough. That was never true.

Healing and new life usually don't happen in a clap of thunder. Like most worthwhile things, they may take time, commitment, effort, and practice. For the sake of healing, our soul may take us to places our consciousness doesn't want to go, and may take us there again and again so that we may have however many opportunities we need, to heal and transcend.

There is no one formula for how to heal. Your path is your own, and your surest guide is the still small voice within you. You can be sure that the process of healing will include some rock-bottom honesty, patience, and forgiveness in many places along the way. Remember to be kind to yourself, and to respect and honor your soul's choices.

I wish I could tell you that I have healed myself so totally that now I never have any problems at all. Not so. Problems are life's opportunities. The purpose of life is the journey, not the destination, and the great secret is that life does not have a destination because it does not have an end. Life is infinite; learning is infinite too. Please enjoy every inch of the road.

Every wound will heal. Every earnest step is a soul-success that takes you forward. Nothing can take you back. Life will present exactly the lesson your soul needs at exactly the time you need it. Even when it seems to be not what you want, it is what you need. Even if you feel you are not ready to handle it, you are. The universe is yours to explore. and you never have to handle it alone.

7. You Could Choose Peace

The tragic and shocking events of September 11, 2001 brought unimaginable destruction and the deaths of more than 6,000 people. Nothing like that has ever happened here before, America has been blessed with peace ever since the end of the civil war, a tragic war whose purpose was to keep the promise of our world-shattering Constitution which said, "All men are created equal" even though most of the writers of that otherwise brilliant document did not understand what that meant, at the time.

There has been no land-war in the continental U.S. since the 1860s, but now the world is very different. The risk of violence and hate and greed for power are growing all over our small planet, and today's wars are utterly, unimaginably, more horrible and more lethal, not just to countries, but to the human species. We have plenty of good reasons to be afraid. But fear stokes more conflict, and wars never end wars. The vicious circle goes round and round. A child once asked, *"What if they gave a war and nobody came?"* There has never been any statement more profoundly brilliant than that, and the very next thought in the minds of the wise of every age was, *"Why don't we try something different?"*

In this little part of the world where I sit, thinking, all is quiet. I have some work to do, but first, I deserve to linger over my morning coffee, here on the back porch in a patch of sunlight. Leaning back against the wooden porch rail, I'm taking some time for myself, a vacation from the stress for a while. Not worried, not obligated., not "productive."

I'm taking time to be a free and natural animal. I am surprised to find that this simplicity and gentle pleasure is still here for me, even with the world as it is. I feel so grateful. This is a holy moment. In this moment, in spite of everything, I feel at peace, and I recognize that this is a gift.

Peace covers me lightly and gently like the morning sunshine. Just in this moment, in spite of everything, I am not afraid. I could be – my life and the lives of friends and family have been profoundly shaken and changed this year by illness and death in our personal world. Yet, somehow, after weeks and years of fears, just in this moment a little window of truth has opened up, and somehow, I am done being afraid. Maybe not forever, but for now.

Here on the back porch it's Indian Summer Sunday morning. I didn't go to church today, but I know that God is everywhere with me, all the time, and I don't have to go to His place of business to connect with Him. In fact, I can never be unconnected from what God Is. *He is here.*

Filtering through the leaves of the oak tree, speckled sunlight and shade scatter pretty patterns across my T-shirt and my arms. I begin to notice things, like the joyful innocent little lives around me.

A squirrel scampers gingerly along the top of the fence like a tightrope walker, from the sycamore tree to the garage roof. The sparrows in the bushes are busy at their commerce, while my lazy garden, sprouted with weeds and dandelions, dozes content in the Autumn sun. And then suddenly– *a hummingbird!* Magical, impossible, glistening, vibrating tiny creature! It darts closer to visit the potted pink geraniums on the porch. It has no fear of me. I am not dangerous, and she knows this somehow.

Not very far away the freeway rumbles softly with its constant roar of engines and the sounds of rubber tires on pavement. But here, even in the roar, there is a quietness, and somehow, amazingly, there is peace. Just in this moment, I feel safe and I know I am loved.

Whatever else is going on, out there, over there, where human beings kill and torture each other, and all of them are claiming that God is on their side, and many of them are saying that they are doing this for the glory of *(fill in the blank with some name/version-of God).* Through it all, God looks on with gentle patience, immeasurable sorrow, and infinite love for Her foolish children.

There is only one God, no matter how many names and forms we create for ourselves to try to own God, or to try to understand. He/She does not belong to some of us and not to others; we all belong to God. God has not parceled Himself/Herself up into different pieces with different names to fight against Himself/Herself like that. War and killing– none of this is God's idea or God's will, and to call it that, surely must be a mistake. How can it be that so many people believe in killing as a way to win peace? My heart asks the silence of the morning.

We know in every religion, that God has given us free will, and free choice. These are the terms of employment for the job of Human Being on planet earth. Whatever we choose, God's universe provides. He who lives by the sword, dies by the sword, and a heart that hates can never be happy. Somehow, every insane murderer has convinced himself that he is right, that he is the good guy killing the bad guy. But we don't have to be insane too. We have a choice.

And so I have chosen peace, for here, for now. The beauty of God's wondrous world is glory enough for me, and fame enough, and power enough. Here in the back yard on this little street of honest, hardworking multi-hued good-neighbors, God's beautiful world lives in quiet glory, with dogs barking and kids laughing and glittering autumn sunlight and astonishing grace.

8. What Is New Thought?

Surely one of the biggest challenges in life is to live your faith even among people who have different visions of what a life of faith should look like. Though I've attended many Churches, I was raised in the Methodist Church and my family were all devoted church members. Sunday mornings, rain or shine, Mother got us all up early, washed and dressed in Sunday clothes, and all three generations of us trooped off to church together.

We had a truly gifted and soul-inspiring minister. He spoke eloquently in simple understandable words that gave us a practical, livable vision of faith and good works. That vision has stayed with me throughout my life, and is still the basic template of all my ethics and actions.

The members of my family still attend traditional churches. Although they are good people every day of the week, their faith is strongly defined by the structure, style, and physical form of the churches they attend on Sunday, and they strictly limit their thoughts about God to the views of their minister and the church's official dogma.

My younger sister is very devoted to her church, active in all its activities, giving hundreds of hours a year to the dedicated volunteer work she does there. This is the rock-solid faith folks used to call "Old Time Religion." It is her vision of what a true faith should be, and she lives out that faith every day, just as our Mother did, and taught us all to do also. I consider myself very fortunate to have had this strong foundation of faith.

I have lived a long time since then. In traveling the path of my own life, I've had many experiences, made mistakes, had successes, failures, joys, disappointments, sorrows, physical challenges, unexpected blessings, and new beginnings. I have come to a broader and deeper truth for my own life, a deeper and clearer unity with The Presence/ God/ the universal consciousness that is the author and loving caregiver of everything that is. Now my personal spiritual vision is wider than that of my family's tradition.

One of the New Thought faith denominations is the Unity movement. It began just over a hundred years ago, starting as a Christian prayer group in the parlor of a middle-aged couple in Missouri, and now has reached throughout the world. Unity is one of a number of New Thought faiths which developed in the late 1890's.

I'm about to make a trip home to visit relatives and old friends I haven't seen in years. We've never talked much about the spiritual aspects of our lives. I know that when I go home this time, I may be called upon to testify to my faith, so I sat down this morning with my journal and my coffee to think about what the differences are, and how I might explain the new ideas that my faith embraces.

The very first thing I realized was that these ideas are not new at all. The truths and basic tenets of the Unity Faith and New thought are actually ancient. Most of the same principles can be found in the Koran, the Talmud, the Upanishads, and the New Testament. These basic principles are also in many other religions too, including Buddhism, Taoism, Hinduism, and more. You might say that New Thought was born of the discovery that ancient and modern faiths do not actually contradict each other in essence, only in the forms and rules human beings have clothed then in.

With that as a starting point, I set out to find and write what the differences are between my personal faith and the the Old Time Religion of my family and past generations, and where they come together. I will say, up front, that I do not speak with any authority whatsoever or from any written doctrine. I don't speak for any group or movement. What I have written here is simply to be shared with whoever finds it meaningful and resonant with their own inner wisdom. I write this from my heart, and from my personal faith and vision. I have no special knowledge, only my own personal relationship with God and the infinite, just like you.

For every human being, I believe it is a part of our work and journey here to seek and find our personal truth in our own lives. Your vision of faith may be different from mine; that is not a problem or conflict. New thought respects all sincere religions, all faiths, all sentient beings, as part of God's plan for us. We travel different paths to the same goal. So, for my family and all else who want to know, here is my vision of New Thought, and my truth as my heart and mind see it:

1. We are all, in fact and function, daughters and sons of God, and more than that. We are God expressing in the world. That is the ultimate truth, the essential tenet of the New Thought/ New Paradigm. There is no way out of this truth, no matter what we choose to believe, or choose to do in this life. Even if we choose to *not believe* in God, we can't make God stop believing in us.

2. The God of the Universe is a loving God who does not punish us for our mistakes, and who loves each soul and each person unconditionally, no matter what we do, or what we don't do. No one is ever abandoned by God.

3. All truths are fully functional, whether we choose to recognize them or not, and nothing is hidden from us. Everyone who earnestly seeks, will find, and what we ask believing, we receive.

4. The God who created us gave us the unlimited power of free choice. The spiritual Laws of the Universe always give us what we ask for, regardless of whether we are consciously aware what we are asking.

5. We have the power to shape and create our lives

and circumstances, and in fact we are always doing so, every one of us, whether we recognize this truth or not. One of the primary endeavors of all New Thought faiths is to become conscious of the choices we are making, and to make choices that are in harmony with our soul, rather than by habit, the logic of the intellect, the shallow needs of the ego, or the emotions of the passing moment.

6. There are no accidents, and we are not bound by "luck" or "fate." Our experiences are chosen by our own souls so that our physical mortal self can have goals, challenges, and learnings to experience while we are here on this earth at this time. To grow our soul is why we are here.

7. Every challenge is a gift, no matter what the material outcome, because each one is an opportunity to learn and grow in Spirit and closer conscious union with God and Life.

8. When we seek to follow the counsel and guidance of God/our soul//the Christ within, we are guided surely, and provided for generously. However we are always free to follow our intellect, our ego, or the advice of others instead of listening to the voice in our hearts. We can hurt ourselves and others unless and until we realize there is a happier way, and then we make the decision to change those choices.

9. A big difference between New Thought from Old Time Religion is that we as Children of God are expected to grow, and have a responsibility to eventually "grow up." We are here to learn, and to become less like children and more like God (or Christ, depending on your specific form of faith.) That's a big task and a huge responsibility, which is one reason why so many of us cling to the comfortable and familiar safety of the old ways, believing that if we're good children, that's enough.

And in a way, it is. God/the Universe loves, accepts

and supports whatever we choose to do with the gifts and the life we've been given. We will not be punished if we don't take the risk to go forward into a calling we hear but are afraid to follow. After all, it is sure to be different from what we have known, and it won't be a well-marked, well-lighted super highway like the traditional way. God and Spirit will be "a lamp unto our feet," but the path may be narrow, sometimes hard, and lighted only a little portion at a time.

10. No one walks this path of spiritual growth alone, and those who find the courage and trust to follow it are creating the future of faith for all of us.

11. The old-way was "follow the leader." This is also a game children play. The new way/new thought is not really new; it has been told by the greatest of spiritual Teachers of every age. It says, "You are the light of the world." In essence: "You are the leader; you have the Buddha and the Christ spirit within you. You can at any time choose to make the commitment to walk the walk, to live the life, and accept your sonship with God."

12. Taking responsibility for our lives gives us the power to change them. All actions and attitudes follow thoughts, and life evolves from this. When we take charge of our thoughts, choosing consciously and intentionally, we are taking charge of our lives. We can then dedicate a life of great power and service to the work our soul came here to do.

13. The answer is always within. The guidance you need is within, the light is within, the connection to God is not in the synagogue, the church, the temple, the mosque, or any group or place or time, the connection to God is within you. It is always available, anywhere, 24 hours a day, forever.

14. New Thought faiths, like most of the world's faiths, believe in reincarnation and eternal life. What's real

of us, and eternal, is not the personality or the physical body of us, but the immortal spirit. This lifetime is temporary, but it is unique in all eternity, never to be repeated, and therefore sacred.

15. As the sons and daughters of God, our highest human goal must be to accept our inherent divinity within, and express it in this world. We can't can't see the whole journey in advance; we can only see it one step at a time. That's where faith comes in. Trusting God, and trusting ourselves.

One of the hardest learnings for me was a message from my still small voice within that said "You know you are Mine; Claim your power." I didn't want to "go there." I had seen cruelty in people who have power. I wanted no part of that, and feared that if I claimed "my power" I might misuse it too.

It took a few decades of seeking, stumbling, and growing, for me to learn that this power is an expression of *our God-given inner strength,* and this strength is neither good or bad bad in itself. It can open more opportunities to be fair and generous, brave and kind, but like every gift, it depends on how we choose to use it.

A basic principle of New Thought is that everything counts. What you do and what you don't do, what you think and feel. New Thought faith does not focus on man-made rules about placing blame and guilt. Instead it requires taking the personal responsibility to accept and acknowledge that your life and circumstances have been primarily created by you, not by other people or by circumstances, or even by a judging or punishing God. They have been called forth by your spirit to challenge you, and to give you obstacles and experiences to learn from. You are never a victim of "fate" or "luck." There are no "outside" forces, only those that you have called forth into your life, even though unknowingly. Therefore it is important to be conscious and aware of the choices, large and small, that you are making each day of your life.

This is a large responsibility. It can be a frightening unless you also accept the strength, the gifts, the guidance, the calling, and the sonship. This is not about religion, it's about everyone's personal relationship with God. This is the only thing God asks of us.

In many traditional religions, we were told to see ourselves as servants of God, stewards of His fields, sheep of His pastures, and His children. The new faith that will take us into the future of planet earth, if there is to be one, will require that we grow up. That will mean accepting our sonship, our inheritance, our share of responsibility, and our individual calling.

Traditions are priceless. They have brought us this far. Truth is eternal, and the only thing that's changing now is that humanity has begun to see some truths that a great many of us had not recognized or acknowledged before. They are the same truths Jesus taught 2,000 years ago, but we didn't "get it." We didn't realize that He actually meant what He said. He was onto something that shook the foundations of the world, and He came here to share it.

When He said "I am the light of the world" and then he said "You are the light of the world." I thought he was talking to the disciples. When I found out he was saying that to me, it changed everything.

He is saying that to you. Old-Time Religion says: "Let others tell you how to live." New Thought faith says: "Live your life knowing the truth that you have been given the choice, the responsibility, the gifts, the guidance, and the power to live your life profoundly."

9. Who Do I Want To Be?

Who am I? That's the question every human being asks at some point in life. We ask it frequently and earnestly, but it has to be asked again and again, for we are growing and changing. The bigger question as we live our lives every day is Who do I want to be? For we are always becoming.

Our days and experiences seem to come and go like the weather. Some days the clouds overcast the sun, but what happens on the dark days is equally as important as what happens in the sun. The hard times of our lives, the times we stumble, the challenges, successful or not, create who we are and who we will be. *We are shaped by our experiences, but we are not defined by them.* Our true value lies neither in our successes nor our mistakes.

In every challenge, we have the choice of resistance or surrender, holding on or letting go, but also the most powerful choice of all, transcendence.

Marianne Williamson described this in a beautiful way: "Rise above the battlefield, strong and magnificent." I read this at a time in my life when I was not strong enough to battle the forces surrounding me, helplessly trapped in what was intended to hurt and damage me. There was no recourse, no defense, and no escape. But I was able to survive when I realized that *I had the choice to refuse to play the empty game.*

It was really a game of pride and ego. Of the ones who would defeat me, I realized that *I did not want to be like them if that was what it took to "win."* I was not always strong enough to win the battle, but I was brave enough keep my integrity, and face my "failure" with dignity. In doing that, I saw that regardless of opinion, I truly did win. Time would vindicate me, and karma would reward my oppressors and myself with what we each had earned.

There will be times in your life when you will stand stronger than you thought you could, and fight the fair fight, honestly and courageously. But there will also be times when the battle is unworthy of you.

In the midst of it all, your emotions will blast you like a hurricane, and it will be very hard to see things clearly. In those times, your heart knows, and will tell you the truth, even among all the shouting voices around you. Your inner truth will always speak quietly but clearly.

Take a different perspective, if only in imagination. Rise above the scene of the problem or the abuse, and look down on it it from there. Is it really worthy of your time and integrity? If not, you have the right to decline the game. stand calm in the wind, face it no matter how unfair or untrue, and let it pass. Your path will continue without pause.

Physically we are born helpless and innocent, with everything to learn. it may take half a lifetime to learn that we are not helpless spiritually, but in fact we are very powerful beings, who can and do shape our own lives, once we know the secret that we are building our own lives not only with our actions– those are only secondary– but with our sense of Self and our beliefs and expectations from life– those are primary. Then we begin to live with a wider view, and recognize higher options. When we decide to rise above the battlefield, and we consciously choose who *we want to be, who we know we truly are, not as the world sees us, but as God sees us*, then nothing on earth can keep us from becoming it.

10. Mission and Purpose in Life

In God's plan, nothing is wasted. Even that which seems lost, is not. Even that which seems unimportant, is not. God always gives us more than we need, and many paths to choose from.

Look around you at the incredible variety of nature. Did God really need so many kinds of butterflies? So many shapes of leaves, so many glorious colors of wildflowers? For any practical purpose, *no.* God created this beautiful abundance everywhere, because God is generous and loves abundance, and so gives abundance to us.

Of all His creatures, we are surely his most unusual experiment. As far as we know, we are the only creatures to whom God has given the gifts of free will, choice of destiny, and the power to create physical reality with our minds and manifest it in our world. With these gifts comes an inner desire to express God with them, and this is what calls us to seek our mission and purpose in life.

We all have the same purpose, and we know this in our soul. It is to create and live a meaningful life wherever we are, here on earth. The primary tasks of this purpose are to grow, to learn, to heal, to create, to teach, to love, to nurture, and to share all of it with our co-journeyers here. All of these tasks are non-finite; they have no "done" point.

Mission, though, is finite, it's a calling that is specific. For Mother Teresa, it was to love the lost, to gather and nurture the unwanted of a particular people in a particular place - the place where she found herself in life. It was not "out there." She did the ordinary things that she saw were needed, and she made them holy with her dedication and her love. Her well-known answer when asked about her important work was this: "We can do no great things, only small things with great love."

Your mission might be somewhere in a distant land, something you may not feel prepared for and yet you feel called by your heart to do. It may be something in the public eye, very visible and grand, or something very private, known only in your own heart. It could just as well be that your soul's mission is right where you are now, even doing what you are already doing, but in a larger, deeper, more conscious way. Anything can be holy, when it is truly and sincerely dedicated to being so.

For many of us, when we look at life in a conscious way, we may realize that we want to change what we do, or change how we do it, because it may not be enough to satisfy the deep quiet inner urging of our soul. That's when we begin to look for a way to work that seems more meaningful and gives us the feeling that we matter, that we are giving something to our world. The change we make doesn't have to be geographical, but it is large, and it is real, inside of us.

For many years I was searching for "my dharma," my mission in life. I must have been looking for some vaulted calling, some special assignment from God that only I could do, which would glorify God and help to enrich other lives and the world. I went to my prayers and to my Spirit Within, and asked to be shown My Mission. Again and again I kept asking and not knowing, until one day I got this message:

"Your work is revealed to you day by day. Everything you do and everything you say is part of it. Any work is an opportunity. All of life is opportunity... But there is work we have chosen to do together. Seek to know it, and when you know it, put it first above all else, and I will prosper it."

"Aha!" I thought, "There IS one destiny for me! But what is it?" and I found myself right back at square-one.

Eventually I realized that we can be called to more choices, and far more opportunities than one lifetime can use, and always there are many possible destinies for each one of us.

God/ Universal Consciousness does not set a riddle or a treasure-hunt and then send us into this world of physical limitations to blindly search for it, while we live in frustration and fear of missing the mark. Instead we are given an abundance of choices, and we are free to choose from our heart's desire, and even, to choose again.

The message I bring to you this day is simply this: Give yourself permission to live one day at a time. Honor every honest effort you make, honor and respect the work you do, and the events of this day and every day you are here as if they are sacred, because *they are*.

You are always a work-in-progress. If you have been pushing yourself to serve God in the best possible way, ease up on the pushing. It's probably not necessary.

What is necessary is that you accept and receive the spirit that is trying to flow through you, and let it flow out into whatever you do, whoever you are now. The flow will carry you to wherever you need to go, and you will become what you need to be, to express God in your life in the fullest and most personal way.

> *"You know not what the harvest is.*
> *There is more than you can see.*
> *Trust and know that no honest work*
> *is without harvest,*
> *and no earnest effort*
> *goes unnoticed by God."*

11. The Gift of Now

My sleep lately is crowded with dreams, but when I wake, I can't remember them. It feels as if I've just arrived home from a short but complicated trip to another time-zone, one that has left me anxious and disoriented. My dreams disappear because they reflect my waking life– too busy with too much. As soon as possible I must file it all away and constantly "clear the desk" to get ready for all the things I know will flood in again immediately.

These days I have an inner urge to simplify my life. I have begun to clear out some of my many stacks and shelves of books and papers and binders of information. For every piece, there was a reason to keep it, so I saved it, provided it with shelter and maintenance rent free, for years, even decades. I was always struggling to catch up, to get past the pile of undone tasks from yesterday, so that I could finally get to the luxury of living right now, today.

I had saved all these books and notebooks crammed with information and resources in case I might need them someday. I saved them and carefully filed and cataloged hundreds of reams of paper for someday when I might need them. Well, *now it IS someday, and I don't need them.*

And so bit by bit, bagful by bagful, I am sorting, un-cataloging, and dispersing them out of my living-space. Now that about 35% of this "stuff" has been given away or thrown away, so far I have not missed any of it. I needed the space much more than I needed the stuff. Some of it was valuable stuff, but its value lay in my past or else in someone else's future. I have untangled and unloaded a large mass of the past and future out of my house, out of my space, out of my mind, and out of my life. Hallelujah! I have room for Now.

I consider the meaning of Now. I've read that "The present moment is the point of power." This is true.

Now is also the Great Unknown, a mystery. I knew this, even when I was a child, but what I know about *Now* that I didn't know then, is that Now is the only real time that exists, ever did, or ever will. I know it, even though I still get stuck in that catching-up mode again, feeling like I'm running behind, I'm not doing enough, fast enough.

Yet my inner wisdom, lately confirmed by quantum physics, knows there is no real time, only the concept of it as a container. What I'm striving to do is to get past it and break free into Now.

It may be that the only way to be truly free from the tyranny of the myth of past and future with its unfulfilled hopes and intentions is to simply throw them all away. Seriously– forgive whatever needs forgiving, and cast all the rest away as if worthless.

But there is something in human beings that makes us hold on fondly to the past, its events and feelings, because we love them, or hate them, or because we fear to let go of them and stand empty at the threshold of the present moment without a map, without a textbook, without a cheat-sheet, without a clue.

Now is almost never what we wish it would be, so we frequently make the mistake of letting it go by while we focus our thoughts on the visions of the future and the memories of the past. We waste a lot of valuable life-time in that way.

We can't change the past because it's gone, and we can't change the future at any other time except now in the present. What we do now always determines what kind of future unfolds for us.

The past is useful for learning things, and for seeing trends to show us what we need to change. But once the lesson is known, put the book away, you don't need it.

I want to let go of the past. dead events, dead issues, even the good parts, knowing that whatever future I will have, I am building now in the present moment. If I want a different future, I can not build it on anything in the past. And yet ironically, logically that is exactly what we have all been conditioned to do. The real value of the past is that we can learn from it, and if we do not learn the lessons of the past and move on, we are doomed to repeat them.

To come truly into the present doesn't mean cutting off all relationships or memories, but it means severing the spiritual bondage to the past. To live in the present means trusting yourself and trusting God. To live in the present is Freefall.

Now calls to me, fascinates and haunts me just as it did when I was that little child who looked up at the darkening twilight sky and wondered deep thoughts like *"What is God?' "What is death like? and Where do we go from here?"* And in those brief moments of innocent wonderings, I experienced eternity. It was something I could not comprehend, but could, just for that moment, know. When we become truly still, truly here, fully aware in the present moment, we experience eternity.

Now is still and always will be The Great Mystery. Now is the portal to the vast unknown. It is the wing of the plane from which we must jump again and again, for all of our life and eternity, and trust that the parachute will open. And I have learned that It is well not to carry too much baggage.

Now is the eternal brink of everything that will ever be. The choices we must make in every moment of this eternal present will create everything that will ever come, or ever be, in our lives. Yet we must make these decisions without any advance knowledge or guarantee of what the results will be. All we can know is that if our thoughts and actions today are kind, Life's response to us will be kind. This is an immutable law, like the Law of Gravity, which is what holds the universe together.

If we could see the future, there would be no reason or need to live here on earth at all. But we will never see the future because it does not exist. Our thoughts, even more than our actions, are creating it now.

Our epiphany is the realization of that truth. Our destiny is the living of it, whether we know it or not.

12. Has God Forgot?

I remember wondering about God when I was ten, so my Granny taught me a simple kind of faith that I could understand, that made me feel safe and loved. She said God was all around me like the air and the sky, only bigger. I knew the sky was forever, so I figured God must be too, and I knew He was around me all the time.

Now that I am grown, I confess I don't know any more about "what God is" than I did then, and that was as good an explanation as anything I've learned since. I was sure that I was safe, sure that I was loved.

I know God is still around, but now sometimes I have confusion, doubts and uncertainties about how this whole God-thing works, because the world I live in now is such a terrible mess.

I've studied spiritual texts, the profound words of mystics and Master teachers who have said that we all have power over our own lives, whether we realize it or not, through the choices we make and their intentions. This is a scary responsibility. When the things or events I want, and believe I need, still evade me, I worry that maybe I'm getting it wrong. When I ask for help in prayer and it doesn't seem to come, I wonder, Has God forgotten about me? And left me here on my own, the same way others in my life have done? I knew it wasn't because they didn't love me, but they just forgot, or they were too busy. And now I can't help thinking, *well, God is really, really busy with a universe to run.*

Then I have to remind myself: *God doesn't forget.* There's enough of God for everyone, and God has an eternity of time. God still listens to every child's secret wish and hears every soldier's silent prayer. No one of us is alone. As long as the sky is, so is God, only bigger.

13. The Positive Bias of God

The universe has a positive bias, says Unity Minister Rev. Robert Trowbridge. He also said you and I and everything in the universe are not only created by God, but we are also actually created *out of* the very substance and essence of God. *"We are all made out of God-stuff"* he says, and since everything that exists is made out of God-stuff, God is in all things, and all beings.

From the beginning, God gave us free will. God lets us hurt ourselves if we choose to. (And it's important to recognize that it's "choose to" which may or may not mean "want to.")

I believe that God's universal laws definitely tend to support and assist considered choices, loving actions, and positive endeavors more than the destructive things we pursue at lesser moments in our lives. Sometimes we are saved by Grace in spite of ourselves, nevertheless the power to help or harm is in us, because the gift is already given. God lets us have our own way.

Here's the good news: We have free will. And now here's the bad news: We have free will. We all manifest our lives through the thoughts and beliefs that we hold in consciousness, even when we don't realize them.

God's universe is a conscious, listening, watchful and responsive universe. It is One Mind. At its creative Source, everything we see, perceive, and think we know as solid material, is Mind. This is the basic premise of all New Thought faiths and studies, and more recently, quantum physics. But there's a "catch-22" that can keep us from having happy lives: we are often *"unconscious."* We are unaware what we are really thinking, believing, and creating. Unaware that all these thoughts and beliefs profoundly influence our life and the circumstances we are calling forth to ourselves. This is that "truth that makes us free." We all have this life-gift and creative power, and its laws are in effect at all times. We are creating our own lives whether we know it or not, and so, when we know, we can create more of what we want. The key is awareness.

Sometimes we make bad choices and find unhappy circumstances playing out in our lives, and we may say "I guess it was God's will." This is the classic cop-out. We are refusing to take responsibility for our own influence on our lives. This does not change the immutable laws of the universe, which are unchangeable.

The truth is, everything that comes, comes to bless us and teach us. We are not helpless pawns of fate, and not victims of other people. When we recognize and accept this truth, we take rightful dominion over our lives. We release and put to use the Christ-Spirit that was always within us.

This is a critical recognition: we are co-creators with God. We are active participants in how God shows up in the world. With the acceptance of responsibility for our part of creating our life up to now, *not all, but our part,* comes the power to re-create it differently. As soon as we commit and begin, God/the Universe moves too, with unexpected and often unseen events and circumstances to facilitate and empower our endeavors.

The key that opens unlimited possibility and makes that power available to us is the acceptance of the truth that *we have it.* We have always had it, because that's the way the spiritual universe works.

Taking personal responsibility for the life you have instead of blaming others, fate, luck, or God, empowers you to create the life you want. You can begin at once, changing the life you have into the life you want.

This will not be effortless. There is something in us

that fiercely resists change, even change for the better. There was some self-protective reason why we made those earlier choices in the first place. Maybe it seemed easier at the time, and safer. Or sometimes we made those choices because someone else thought we should, or told us we must. The oldest excuse: "I have no other choice" is also a choice. You are just choosing to deny choosing. You have chosen to be helpless and powerless, and thus have called that condition into your life. The truth is that you, and all of us, always have another choice. No matter where you are in your life now, there is someplace else to go.

Don't let anyone else choose your life for you, they can't. Only *your choices* shape and form *your life.* Contrary to appearance, your life is really created from the inside out. That is where Spirit lives in you, and from there expresses into the world AS you. The thoughts, actions, and choices of other persons do not really affect your life, except to the degree that you allow them to influence your beliefs, and so your choices.

You don't have to let other people's beliefs about you become YOUR beliefs about you. You don't have to let other people's choices become your choices, even though the right choice may be harder.

I believe that we have a responsibility to God to be joyful, generous, prosperous and happy, loving and loved. I'm convinced that this is what God wishes for us. But what we think and believe becomes the functional truth of our life. *We set the sails; God provides the wind-power,* reliable, steady and kind. If we set a poor course and our ship takes us there. It's not the fault of the wind.

Get on-purpose, and follow the quiet voice in your heart. Whatever you seek, you will find. Be aware of what you are seeking.

14. The Soul-Mind

I've been alone a lot in my life, not by choice I thought, but it just "went that way." It may be that some of us are meant to walk much of our way alone. Some solitude is necessary and healthy, and a quiet life does provide a lot of time to think, and a wider uncluttered perspective with which to discover the world and life, to be aware that we are discovering it, and to realize that in so doing, we are creating it for ourselves. This is the gift in it: becoming aware.

We live always on two levels that we know of. They are the Physical of our humanity, and the Metaphysical of our divinity. There are probably many more that we can't see or know yet with only the human mind.

Very early in my life I was aware of something like this, and at first I didn't question it. Even as a child I had a sense of mystical things, but I didn't know what to do with that. From the grownups I learned to doubt myself, and I began to accept what other people said, and what they believed instead of my natural spirituality of a child.

We all do this,. We are tribal animals who naturally live in groups and seek to match each other in order to be safe. We're designed this way, while we are here on earth. There is a physiological need to feel attached to sameness and Community.

Our science tells us that we are the highest of the animals, because we have a powerful, logical, practical, creative mind and a concept of God. We have historically assumed that other creatures, rocks, and trees, do not. We have long believed that these things do not have any awareness or consciousness like we do, although lately our science is discovering that we have been somewhat mistaken about that.

A friend of mine, a practicing Buddhist, told me, *"You are not your mind."* He meant that the surface-mind is not the same as the soul-mind. He said the mortal mind can be a useful tool or it can be a wild monkey, racing in random circles, ever trying to escape its cage.

"But the soul is always silent and calm, and in that sanctuary within, you are always safe. Get out of your mind and go there instead, and there you will find the answers you seek. Everything in life is yours to have and to know; there is really only the one question: What will you choose?"

But, I insisted, "If I have everything in life, how is it that I sometimes feel so alone? Of this he said,

"Beneath what our physical eyes see, we are only one world. We are only one being. We are only one Life, manifesting in endlessly different forms. This is who we really are: we are this Life, this is why we matter. It cannot be otherwise. Every soul belongs, every soul matters."

What if, in true reality, no one is more alone than anyone else? What if we are only being separated by the misunderstanding and limitations of our humanness, and yet we are all joined by the God-ness that is within us too?

My friend said, *"Separation is an illusion."*

I know this, sometimes I can see it clearly, beneath the pretend-ness of it all, which is the surface of the wave which we mistake for the ocean. And yet, it's an illusion we must live with here, in order to have this adventure and play this game and learn what we have come here to learn.

"The time will come for everyone," my friend said, *"to stop being only a Child of God, and begin to become a Disciple. For many, it may not come in this lifetime."*

15. Life Science for Beginners

When you were born into the world, you had to take whatever you got. You didn't have any choice or awareness yet. All you knew was: "I am here now, and this is what life is." Everything you saw and heard and experienced next, you assumed that it was true.

You grew a bigger body and a bigger mind, and soon an awareness of *other*. You discovered things, and you wanted them. By age two you began to learn that you didn't always have to just take what you got, some things were negotiable. Words began to collect in your head and you noticed they were useful. This was a turning point. Now you could ask for things instead of just crying. This was great! With words, you learned how to willfully influence your world.

You didn't always get what you wanted by asking, so next came the discovery of demanding things, (or as Granny called it, throwing a hissy-fit.) You cried and got down on the floor in the grocery store aisle, kicking and yelling to get that candy bar Mommy said No to. This was another turning point. If *this way* of getting what you wanted worked well for you, your life still might not, and probably, would not.

Parents are our first powerful teachers. Whatever they gave you, that was what you learned to expect life to give you. What we learn in the first five years of our lives create and embed our lifelong subconscious core-beliefs. If you're given too much, that's not good, because you learn to believe you deserve to always get your way, and when life fails to match your expectations, (as of course it must) you tend to carry a resentment against people, life, and authority of any kind, maybe for all your life.

But what if your parents give you too little? With too many No's to your asking? Then you may come to see yourself as undeserving of the things you want. Then, pleading and even tantrums will fail, and you will learn that you're supposed to settle for less and suffer in silence.

Soon life circumstances will begin to teach you the concept of more-than vs. less-than (which is actually an abstract, a perception, not a fact). And you find yourself swimming in a river of truths-and-lies all mixed together, in a whirlpool of subconscious beliefs.

Things get even more complicated in the turbulent teens, when everything you've learned becomes open to question and rebellion, accompanied by new emotions like love, jealousy, sadness, hope, rage and uncertainty. Things taken for granted in childhood will now be opened up to uncertainties in the wider world you must navigate now. There is questioning of everything. This is good. It informs your growing consciousness and you begin to establish a concept of Who You Are in relation to others, *an identity*.

This is when we all become painfully aware, acutely unsure of our worth and our value to others, especially peers, and everything out there in the wider world. You and I and all of us suffer and don't realize that everybody we know is feeling the same way. Even the homecoming queen has deep hidden uncertainties about herself.

After high school comes the Rest Of Life. No matter what surface circumstances occur for you now, this is the time of independently applying and testing what you believe, what your life has taught you so far. Now things really get complicated, and will stay that way for the rest of your earthly journey, unless...

The deep task of life is a continuously evolving cycle of growing inwardly, even as your whole world is growing outwardly, physically and materially, at the same time. Mind, as Consciousness, is our connection to the life-source/spirit/God/The Force (or whatever sense or name you use to call that Great Consciousness that runs the universe.) The Dharma of adulthood is the seeking and learning of The Truth. Not just small truths and facts (i.e. girls are just as good as boys) but the Greater Truth of Who and What We Really Are, as creations and creators, as manifestations of God expressing in form. This turns out to be a lifelong task. This is the Truth that your soul within you is always seeking, that Truth Jesus said would make you free. What He said is true; it does.

The trouble is, up to now, the only way any of us have known how to see what God is, came from the forms we knew, things we were taught as children. Heavenly Father, Grandfather, King of Heaven on a throne in the clouds, huge Person that watches, judges, rewards and punishes.

What if God were not like that? What if somebody made that up, our whole notion and understanding of God? Just patched it together the best they could, made out of what they had learned so far? What if, maybe what they believed was not quite true even for them, and is not at all The Truth for us, here, now?

When we're born, our consciousness is newborn too. Our Higher Consciousness, the Christ-Mind of us, is there from the very beginning. It was here before we were born, and it will still be here after our mortal death. *But we don't know we have it.*

To use the power and wisdom and love of God in His world, you've only got to *recognize that you have it,* that you have choices, and that no matter what happens or how it appears, you are greater than circumstances. You need not be held hostage to mistaken childhood beliefs. But they were planted in your innocence, so they have deep roots. In this life, what we believe is what we receive, whether consciously or unaware, *but if we don't know this, what can we do?*

Step-one to change the life you have now, is to take responsibility for it. It's a big step: own yourself. Consider that it might be true that you are as worthy and deserving as anyone, and also no more worthy than anyone else. Consider that they too are operating on beliefs they may not realize.

If people have hurt you or abandoned you, *that was about them,* for their own needs. *It was never about you.* Your worth was created by God, not the world, and your worthiness is secure. The crucial step that gives you the power to live your best life right now is to practice living with intention, consciously awake, and aware.

We are all continuously asking and receiving, whether consciously or unaware, and Life continuously responds. It cannot be otherwise. The life you have now is the one you created through the action of universal laws which you yourself have set in motion. This is how things work here. You have made this life out of whatever came your way, and you can change it with whatever comes your way next.

We profoundly influence all of life around us with the energy of our consciousness. Actions, events, and people happen in response to what we are believing or habitually thinking and feeling. When we rage at the wrongs, more wrongs show up. Hate attracts more hate to itself, and love attracts more love. Feelings of helplessness create actual helplessness. It's not anything outside of you that's holding you, it's the untruths that you're still believing.

There is God-ness in you, a portion that actually is God Who came here cleverly disguised as you in order to have adventures, to experience everything, and see what it's like. Sorrow, joy, courage, failure, success, pain and ecstasy and most of all, love. So that's your job. To Live as you choose. It's that simple. You stand now at the door of "Everything is possible," but the door only opens from the inside. Open it.

16. The Deepest Voice

There's one voice we use for speeches and another one we use for everyday encounters with each other. Then there is a more honest one with which we speak only in our private thoughts and journals and to our closest friends.

But there is another voice that comes from a deeper place, and rarely speaks aloud or in written words. It comes in meditation and in prayer. Beneath that, there may be even deeper ones, deeper than our conscious thoughts can go. Only God knows how many levels of knowledge and feeling are expressing through us that we are completely unaware of in our physical lifetime here.

There is so much more of the human spirit than we can see or even begin to understand. Somehow we know this, maybe not consciously, but with a deeper knowing.

Mostly we accept the limitations of who-we-are-now, as if it's Who We Are, but we instinctively know that we are more. Every soul wants urgently to break through the limitations and obstacles that life seems to bring into our path, or we bring to ourselves. Inherent in the human species is the desire to conquer, to grow through, and to go beyond what we humanly know.

It has been said, and I know it's true, that God/Spirit speaks to each of us in the way that we can personally understand, but it speaks quietly, so sometimes we don't hear it unless we listen. That's where so many of us are right now, trying to hear.

Please God, help me to hear truly, and to understand, so that I can act with conviction, with purpose, with strong desire and intention, and fulfill my soul's mission here. Open my understanding. Show me Who I Am. I need to see. Show me Who I Am, as You see me.

17. From Here Until Forever

Every so often, Life turns me around. Life changes my plans, cancels my reservations, derails my train, and rains on my parade. Life gives me what I need instead of what I thought I wanted. Life is wiser than me, it sees farther ahead, where I can't see, until I look back later. Then I see. Then I can recognize the devastating collapse of my well-laid plan as the blessing it actually was. It was an an act of grace.

Life has turned me around and faced me in the right direction a number of times when I was forging ahead like a 40-car fast-freight train, sure I was headed for success. But where I was trying to go, if I had gotten there, would have proven to be a dead-end for me, body and soul. So instead, Life opened another door I had not consciously chosen, or perhaps not even seen before.

I admit that it was not easy or always clear. I didn't know how I would come through some difficult passages, some soul-challenges, some losses and sorrows. Many times there was uncertainty, confusion, and terrifying fear. I've had my share of lonely times and I surely have had some hard miles traveling.

And yet, time and again, what looked like and felt like a disaster or a devastating failure, turned out to be a magnificent unexpected opportunity of growth, one that I would not have had the courage to choose for myself unless I had been pushed by life or necessity. And when the time came that I had to look inside myself because there was no other place to go, I learned that I could trust what I found there. Down inside the depths of me, I found what everyone finds – the direct connection to God. *All strength, all courage, all help, is waiting for us to discover it there.*

Sometimes Life/God/universe gives me what I need instead of what I thought I wanted. Troubles redirect me, and reconnect me, lovingly if not always gently. Depending on how far I've taken myself off course, there can be some severe pain for me in the turning.

I make mistakes. Life corrects my course, and I learn. God/Life/my soul does not make mistakes. I know this, but because I'm just me and I'm still learning how to see, sometimes it takes a while to see it. I forget that I am God expressing here on earth as me (after all, how could I be all that?) so time after time, I have tripped over my own feet.

Now that I have lived a while, I can look back from the crest of a different hill, and see the landscape behind me stretching out vast and clear and plain. The miles, the storms, the rocks and rivers I stumbled over and struggled through, are beautiful from here. They were the way I have come to be where I am, and I will go on from here until forever.

18. Making Mistakes

Beloved, each time you stumble, you learn. Each time you fall, you get up stronger. You know this is true, and your life is even now being changed by this truth. Continue to dance, even if you think you might fall. I promise you, you are as graceful falling as you are dancing. Falling is just another word you can call dancing, for in truth, the dance of life can only be every step there is.

Go ahead and dance. Remember to trust your self, and be as kind to your self as you want to be to others, for truly you cannot be any kinder or more loving to others than you are willing to be to yourself.

– RM 01.01 .19

19. Moments

When I first began to notice the shadows of time falling across the landscape of my life, this life we never think will change and then it does, I knew my perspective had to change too. At some point we all come to realize our mortality, and we begin to see some things differently.

Although I know that Life itself, the soul, is eternal, I can see that the human lifetime is not. It is temporary, it is one-of-a-kind. Now looking back from farther up the road, the scale of things has become a lot clearer. I know what's important.

The moments we hold longest in our hearts may be some of the smallest ones, the ones unplanned, unsought, and even unspoken. Ones that came and went without explosions of passion or oceans of tears for either their sorrows or their joys.

Things like the warm dusty summer days, lovely lazy afternoons and sweet calm twilights, green rolling hills and cottony clouds climbing vast skies, when we were so young with nothing special to do, and all the time in the world to do it, the unhurried savoring of it. Oh those were the days, we say, and yet we hardly noticed them at the time. And now, 20, 30, or 40 years past, having forgotten the hard parts of it, we can remember how it was to be young, to be beautiful, to be innocent.

Strange how crystal clearly we remember. I would have thought that decades and distance would dull the memory and blur the edges of the images, the moments, and times. It does not. It brings them back to us, sharp as photographs in an album, still unchanged and forever unchanging. Suddenly, shockingly, we realize for the first time how beautiful they were, how beautiful *we were*, and how beautiful and earnest our parents were, or tried to be. Though they made mistakes, some of them were made for our sake.

Many wonderful people have passed through my life. Too many times, I did not know how to know them, and I didn't have the courage to let them truly know me. I sometimes think of them still, wonder how they are, and deeply wish I could see them again. But they are decades away in unknown places now. They have passed through my days and gone on. Would I change the way it was, if I could do it all again? I think not. We did what we could, all of us. All of us came here to learn how to live, and this is the way we learn, by inches, by moments.

When we enter young adulthood, our perspective takes a radical shift from the innocence and carelessness of the child we were, and we begin the task of becoming who we shall be. The gifts of this age of life are courage, confidence, ambition, discovery, and strength. In later years, the perspective will shift again, and the gifts will become different too. We begin to understand more. The important things become more clear, easier to determine and to decide. Now we have a wider expanse to look back on than to look forward to.

Is there anything I'll regret when I reach the point of embarkation from this earth? This place I love so much, and have traveled through all my years, and am only just now finally learning how to navigate?

Not so much really; no big regrets. I've taken some chances. I've made mistakes. I've loved a lot, and did not always get loved back. I trusted life and love, I tried to give what I had to give, imperfectly of course, but the intention was sincere. I think my one regret is that it took me so long to realize how blessed I have been, in spite of my ignorance, errors, my flaws, and my shortfalls. I hope and intend to make good use of the rest of my life to do more, and better, than I have done so far.

I marvel at how beautiful and wonderful is God's marvelous green earth! How incredible it is to be here, playing and learning this game and dance of life. And how precious beyond words were those people along the way who have honestly loved me, and told me so. Oh that makes all the difference– that they took the risk and the moment, to tell me so.

If you love someone, are you sure they know? When you pause to tell them, it only takes a moment, but lasts a lifetime.

20. Do What You Do

*"What you make, no one else will ever make.
What you discover informs the universe.
What you feel expands the love
I have given you to give the world."*
RM 9.18.07

Whatever God is calling you to do, begin now to do it. The way will be opened, and the means will be provided. Take faith in yourself, for God has had faith in you, and the gift is already given. Claim it and let it express through you.

The world is terribly in need of loving enterprise of every kind: honest business, truthful partnerships, and the practice of kindness as a lifestyle. Take a stand for what you know is true. Refuse to do things you feel and know are wrong. Give up the sad excuse that it's okay because "everybody does it." *You're not everybody.* You're a unique, valuable and powerful being in your own right, created that way by the Creator of all that is. You are designing your own life in this very moment, so give yourself full credit for this gift. Be brave and generous, be kind and be mindful of what you are choosing, for whatever you are giving into the lifestream, Life will return to you.

Everywhere we look in our world, there is greed and rage, and it is creating more and more greed and rage and sorrow. We don't have to choose that.

We don't have to respond back to that in the same manner. We don't have to *become like that which we fear*, and hold fear and rage in our minds all the time. That only gives fear and rage more power and more places to grow. We don't have to accept that way of being -It's not who we are. It's not our true Source and Being.

We can be different; we can choose differently. We can simply do what we do, mindfully and heartfully. We can simply be who we are and know that we are good enough just as we are, and growing. We can choose to be the best of ourselves instead of giving in to the worst of ourselves, or trying to be like somebody else. For a great many of us that may be hard in the beginning, but it gets easier with practice, and as soon as the commitment is made, the universe moves immediately to support us, to open doors, to provide whatever is needed, and to work simple miracles on our behalf.

Take faith and step out. Do what you can, no matter how small a thing, to make our world a better and kinder place. Laser-focus your actions, and even more, your thoughts and beliefs. Believe only the best you can about yourself and all others, then forgive the rest and leave it behind you. Let it go. Focus the real power of your conscious thought again and again on the finest things you are, ever have been, and ever can be, and hold firmly to those thoughts until they come true. Then they will.

Because what you believe creates the person you are, always look for the best of yourself, claim it as yours, and nurture it. Use it to create a better life for yourself, one day at a time.

You are, we all are, creating a different world than we have known before, or else we are helping to destroy it. What happens next will be according to our choices. This is not only possible, it is inevitable, and it is time now for each one of us to choose. What you believe and what you do, matters in the scheme of things more than you can ever know. It's not too late to make the difference.

21. Everything That Comes

Everything that comes, goes. Born into this world, we come here as a soul alone, and we will leave here as a soul alone. In the meantime, we are given everything on earth to discover. Where we are now, everything that lives, dies, and nothing here is eternal except the essence of us, the soul, the God part, what the teacher Jesus called "the Christ in you."

On earth and everywhere in the cosmos, all things are constantly changing, moving forward in a spiral path, through cycles of hours, days, years, centuries, or billions of years. We mortal beings have the incredible blessing of being consciously aware of this experience, able to be curious about it, and we have a deep inherent hunger to understand it.

Then we leave here. We go to another place to do another thing. When we go, we leave behind the physical embodiment we no longer need, the garment we have worn while we are here. It is magnificent and miraculous, yet it was always only a garment, temporary.

But the essence of us, who and what we are, is as eternal as God/Spirit/Life itself. The true Being of us takes on new forms of energy to employ, and goes on growing and becoming, though we cannot see it now, or know how it will be. The essence that we are, cannot die, and all that we have learned here, we will take with us to the next way of being. Who and what we are, will always be, and we will continue becoming. What we call death, is not the end and is not a failure, but a natural completion, a graduation, and a new going forth.

You are God's creation, and God is therefore in you. God has put on your face, and wears your clothes, loving and enjoying playing the role of you, experiencing the life of you, here. But you don't know this.

Because God is in us, we have great power, even when we don't know this. God gave you and me and every human being the power of free choice, as well as the power and the means to manifest those choices in our lives, and so we do, either consciously, or more often, unaware. We can choose to love or hate, to help or harm. We can make ourselves happy or terribly unhappy, and God won't stop us, if that's what we choose.

Most of my life, I thought I was here on earth and God was out there somewhere, unreachable from here, all-powerful, and not always fair to everyone. My religion taught me that God would punish me if I sinned. It wasn't always clear exactly what sin was, except that a small one would be like telling a lie, and a big one would be like killing someone. That left a lot of things in between that I wasn't quite sure of.

But God is bigger than that. Now I can see that sin can be something that was not meant to be evil, but was a mistake we made. That's a different way of looking at it, that makes more sense to me.

We may never know the whole truth about what God is. The human mind is not designed for that. The whole truth may be too much to bear, as Jesus told his disciples (according to John 14: 25–27) when he left this earth:

"I have yet many things to say to you, but you cannot bear them now. When the Spirit of truth comes he will guide you into all the truth..."

So the truth is always ahead of us, with more to learn, more to discover.

You and I, every living thing, and every seemingly non-living thing that makes up the earth and the stars and the universe, are all God expressing. Everything that is, is God expressing as consciousness, as form, as energy,

All of it exists at the same time. In fact, in reality there is no such thing as time, it's just a part of the system of illusions we use to help us try to understand life and keep track of things, one thing at a time. But nothing in the universe happens one thing at a time!

Everything that is, is God. A soon as we we realize this, every perspective changes. There is transcendence. It does not come by accident, you must be willing and ready to receive it. It may come like a flash of lightning, flooding your mind and body and everything around you with an almost unbearable light and joy. Or it may come quietly, as a gentle realization surrounded by a limitless ocean of peace, forgiveness, and loving assurance. Whatever way it comes, you will know.

God is all there is, and this means we are that, too. We will all experience this someday, when we wake.

At the hour of passage that we have called death, when we transition from this life into the next experience, everyone awakes. But we don't have to wait that long. The truth is always here, now, and we can know it at any time. We can know the truth, choose it intentionally, and live it. We can BE the truth, right here, now, where we are. *You can be the truth,* right here, now, where you are.

22. What's Important

God loves us thats whats important.
All the rest is not important, its just interesting.

When God does something wonderful for you its not because youre important, its because He loves you.

If God uses you to do something important, its God thats doing it. You are His gardener and you are His garden and thats whats important.

Vickie, age 7

23. Before I Wake

We seem to go through life on earth in a linear path. One day follows another, there is a beginning and an end. There is a past, a present, and a future, set up in a straight-line sequence, with borders that we can cross mentally but not physically. But Life is not really like that.

Time is a construct of mind; an organizing device that helps us to make sense of the vastness of life we cannot fully know. In truth we are eternal Spirit taking form and residence in a physical body for a while, to have the adventures and experiences of human love and human limitations.

The life that we have is not the Life that we Are. The Life that we Are is unlimited and eternal, and much larger than the life we live here on earth. This physical life is our wonderful adventure, a journey of discovery. Physically it has a beginning and an end, but the true life that is ours is not contained in that way.

This physical life is not all there is, but it seems to be all there is right now. It is conceived and captured in the illusion of time, and so we believe it is all we have because it is all we know. We understand that each mortal life is unique and each life has a unique purpose, a reason why we came. Part of each one's purpose here is to learn, to grow in spirit (our true self) and to help each other to learn and grow. The lessons can be simple, but many are complex, that involve hurting and healing, forgiveness and compassion, and even experiences that are painful or ugly. We are given each other to help each other get through.

A part of our purpose is to share and then to pass on whatever material, creative, mental or spiritual gifts we have been given. You have gifts that *only you can give.* I know and believe that each of us has a function and purpose that is essential to the human family of God, and even as we need God, God needs us too.

Whoever you are, whatever you do, you have a calling in this life. You may not have recognized it yet, but nevertheless it is there, and functioning in the order of things. Your life matters, whether you accept and admit that or not.

Every life matters. We are souls who are traveling in timeless eternity, yet we are here in a world defined and limited by time. We are bigger than this life alone. We are much bigger than the day-to-day pursuit of time-bound things, bigger than we can fully understand.

When I was a small child, my grandmother taught me this little prayer:

> *Now I lay me down to sleep;*
> *I pray the Lord my soul to keep.*
> *If I should die before I wake*
> *I pray the Lord my soul to take.*

Even though I was only three years old, these words were sobering to my little mind, and even frightening, because of the idea that (1) I might die and (2) my soul was not safe; I might lose it in the dark accidentally, so I must ask God each night to keep it for me. But even if I asked, could I be sure He would?

Now that I'm grown. I know that God has already made my soul safe. No one can lose their soul, because it is at the depth of who we truly are. We can deny it, and refuse to believe in it, but it cannot be lost, damaged, or sullied in any way. We are not this personality, or this body, or this ego-mind. These are just some of the tools and instruments we have been given to use and to enjoy while we are here on this wonderful and amazing life adventure. It is that deepest Self that is truth, that's who we really are.

We cannot ever lose our soul to the devil, for God has guaranteed our souls for us, eternally ours and eternally His. There is no devil in reality, except the ones we create in our minds to punish ourselves when we forget we are all God's own, and when we fail to trust Him. We do this because we are caught up in the illusions and limitations of the physical world. And yet, we have only to turn to God within us, in any place and any time, and He is there, and Christ has paid every debt we will ever owe. If we ask sincerely, we will be forgiven.

We have free will. That's how it is. We are allowed to make all the mistakes we want, God is not a prison guard, watching us, ready to blame and punish. God is in control, and gives to each one of us as we have asked, whether unconsciously by habit, or consciously by prayer, meditation, or mindfulness. At any time we can speak to and listen to the Still Small Voice of God that is within us, for it is always lovingly listening.

As beautiful as it is, and as terrible sometimes, this physical world does not control us, unless we believe it does. When we believe that it does, we are handing over our spiritual power to something outside ourselves. Then we will act in fear, blindly, helplessly or violently because of our fear, our sorrow, our rage, and our pain.

There is no need to do that. There is another way, and an infinity of choices. But we may get lost in the illusion, like a character in our own dream. Struggling to escape from some terrible danger that is really only a dream, we will stumble and fall and try to run, desperately in slow motion and in terror. Have you ever had a nightmare like this? We dream ourselves into facing horrible dangers, doing terrible things in our nightmares that we would never do awake. Then when we wake up in a cold sweat, we think to ourselves "How could I dream such a thing? and say, "Thank God it was just a dream!"

In our world today, so many of us are living in a state of distorted reality that we believe is real. We believe violence and wars, crimes and atrocities are necessary. Many of us are living this nightmare even though we don't want to. By the power of our thoughts and beliefs, we actualize and manifest these frightening things in our world and in our lives. *We don't have to manifest this - we can manifest anything– whatever we believe, hold in our thought, and and speak in our words. But we must be awake and aware of what we are believing, for that will be what we are creating.*

The great many of us, without knowing, have been programed subconsciously by images, stories, movies, TV and the mass-murder video games we have given to our children just when they are first-learning about life. we don't realize that we are shaping the beliefs that become their subconscious core-beliefs for life. Like, "Killing is okay. Whoever kills the most is the winner..."

Is there is something you are believing right now that you wish were not true? Then *change* your mind. *Decide* to catch and correct your habitual automatic thoughts, from "I can't do anything about it" to what you would rather have in this world. In due time life must respond to your creation, as it is doing right now, and always has done. As John Lennon said, *Imagine.* This alone is enough to send a clear and powerful message to the universal law that is always working and always listening. When our thoughts and beliefs change, the world we experience changes accordingly. That process begins immediately and goes on continuously. This is the basic way God and the Universal Consciousness works.

Changing our habits of thought and belief is no easy task. We may not even notice what we are thinking and believing. To change our mind, we must first open it to the truth. That takes a commitment to trust God and walk in faith. To do that, first we must wake up from the illusion that we "can't help it" and that "It's just the way of the world" or "I'm one person- What I think doesn't matter."

That is the illusion. That is the bad dream. The truth is, your thoughts and your beliefs matter enormously. They have more power than you know, more power than guns, more power than governments. Make no mistake about this, what we believe and hold in thought plays a powerful part in creating the world, minute to minute, hour to hour, and day to day. It determines what we allow and what actions we take, and even more, it influences the Universal Mind of which you and I are a vital part.

The challenge of this life and the times we live in, is to wake up. Accept and take responsibility for the power that you do have. And yes, it is scary to do that, but much more scary NOT to. Many of us will pass through this life, and "die before we wake." Don't let one of them be you.

Everything we really need has been given to us by God. We have been designed and intended to live joyful, peaceful, useful, loving lives here in this beautiful little blue and green garden where our Father has placed us to play. Wake up and see it. All over the earth, ordinary people are quietly awakening, even in this very moment. There is a reason why you came here to this page, these words, on this day in your life. Awake, and help create a different world for all of us.

24. Live Today

At this time in human history there is so much that is ugly and dangerous. There are thousands if images of violence, hatred, and destruction that no child should see, every day and night blasting out of the TV screen into our homes and seeping into our own as well as our children's minds. It is more important than ever before, to choose carefully what things we focus our thoughts on, and what things we give harbor to in our homes and our hearts, unaware.

Whatever we give attention to, positive or negative, grows. Please don't take anything unworthy of you into the center of your consciousness, for whatever you hold and focus on in consciousness, you are giving power to.

> "Whatsoever things are true, whatsoever things are honest, whatsoever things are just, whatsoever things are pure, whatsoever things are lovely, whatsoever things are of good report; if there be any virtue, and if there be any praise, think on these things." Philippians 4:8

This life you have is your soul's chosen adventure. Live it now, with as much love and joy as you can. Not just with pleasure, but with joy- they are not the same.

Don't wait till tomorrow to live and love. Don't wait for things to get better, or until you can afford it. Take a deep breath and look for whatever there is in your life that's beautiful now, however small, and focus on those things so that they can grow. For you are the creator of your life and circumstances, and whatever you give your attention and feeling to, grows and manifests as your life.

Don't live every day of your life on a deadline. Don't rush past your little garden without seeing its untidy small beauties. Notice things. The bitter green color of spring grass, so intense that you can almost taste it, the freshness of the roses spattered with sweet rain. They were put there for you.

Linger after sunset before you turn on the lights. In the twilight there comes a lovely sense of peace, and you might see the flickering of fireflies on a summer night, and the first stars come out.

Life is eternal, but this earthly journey is temporary, unique, and sacred. Live it today. Live it right now, with as much joy as you can. Whatever is happening that is hurting you, let it go. Forgive everybody, and then forgive yourself, and turn back to your joy.

Never pass up an opportunity to be a little bit kinder, a little bit more generous, a little bit more loving. You never know when a little thing as simple as a smile to a passing stranger on the sidewalk might be enough to save a life. Never pass up an opportunity to give love or to accept it.

Life is rich; spend it like a millionaire. Rejoice in it. That's what it was given to you for.

About The Author

V. Blakeman Vaughn is a poet and essayist
living in the Pacific Northwest.
to contact this author:
forever@darkhorsepress.com

About Darkhorse Press

We are a Small Press in the time-honored tradition of American authors and self-publishers like Henry David Thoreau, Ralph Waldo Emerson, and Walt Whitman. Small Presses and self-publishing have always been a respected part of American Literature.

Our writers and publishers are dedicated to the communication of the principles and truths of New Thought and non-denominational practical Spirituality.

www.ingramcontent.com/pod-product-compliance
Lightning Source LLC
Chambersburg PA
CBHW050605300426
44112CB00013B/2082